a
Time of Trauma

How Your Church Can Minister to its Community Through Crisis

Rhona Knight

GROVE BOOKS LIMITED
RIDLEY HALL RD CAMBRIDGE CB3 9HU

Contents

Church Mission Society supports the Grove Mission and Evangelism Series
At Church Mission Society, we believe that every Christian is called to join in God's mission, whether that means crossing the street or crossing continents, and we want to set people free to put that call into action.

Acknowledgments
The author wishes to acknowledge the work of Professor Christopher Southgate and the Tragedy and Congregations Team who supported the Common Awards Seedcorn Grant from which this work emerged.

First Impression February 2021
ISSN 2399-6536
ISBN 978 1 78827 154 7

Introduction

1

> These people, prayerful, humble, faithful, will be the answer…to the question What? What needs to be done here? Who is most at risk? How can we help? Who shall we send? God works in all things *with and through* those who love him.[1]

Mission-related trauma has been considered for a number of years, yet little has been written on the nature of mission in times of trauma. This booklet considers the significant question of practical theology, demonstrating how *trauma care is mission*. Indeed, trauma could be seen as 'the greatest mission field of the twenty-first century.'[2]

Opportunity as well as threat have accompanied the global COVID-19 pandemic crisis. The development of virtual ways of being church saw increased 'attendance' and 'church tourism.' Virtual *Alpha* and other ways of 'meeting' in small groups flourished. Churches put talks and resources online. Practical acts of love and service grew. Foodbanks expanded. Varied forms of COVID-19 care emerged to support those isolated and in lockdown. Christian resources were developed to support healthcare workers, teachers and pupils. This initial flurry of busyness was followed by a lethargy and tiredness. People took stock and began to pace themselves. This was to be a marathon and not a sprint. New patterns of sustainable worship and ministry developed. Some churches returned to meeting physically at the earliest opportunity. Others decided to continue online for the foreseeable future, delivering tablets to those without computers and educating them in their use. Others moved to hybrid church. As finances were threatened, some dioceses furloughed their mission staff and technologically-able curates. Some churches, however, saw increased giving. All this happened against a background of uncertainty, as the pandemic has continued to impact on global physical, emotional, social and spiritual well-being. The COVID-19 pandemic has been a time of complex trauma that has taken the world into uncharted territory. The church spent time in shock, working out how to respond immediately and in the longer term.

Trauma, in varied forms, is part of life, and it is inevitable that we, our communities and our congregations will encounter, negotiate and process trauma. Superficially these appear to be times when the requirement for practical pastoral care is uppermost; to 'use' times of trauma for mission can be seen as a misuse of power. It is sometimes paralleled with giving people a tract when what they require is a roof over their heads and a meal. However, it is not that simple. As Victor Frankl noted, it was choice, hope and meaning, more than bread and clothing, that kept people alive in Auschwitz. Frankl observed that those with a 'why' to live for could bear with almost any 'how.'[3]

In times of trauma it is not enough to deal with physical needs alone

In times of trauma it is not enough to deal with physical needs alone. The normal trajectory through trauma includes the story of trauma being heard and witnessed in a safe space, and that story being reframed within a bigger story as agency is returned and meaning is made. The missional church is well placed to witness these stories and enable protest and lament. Having been denied agency, traumatized people who encounter the omnipotent God have their agency returned. As they encounter the bigger story, meaning can be made from the suffering. This is missional pastoral care, that sees not only the physical needs in times of trauma but sees what else might be done, how else we can help and who else we can send.

The second chapter of this book looks at the nature of trauma, what it is and how it affects the individual. The third chapter looks at the nature of trauma and congregations. It draws heavily on work in America and Britain on tragedy in congregations, particularly the work of Christopher Southgate and his team.[4] Chapter four looks at trauma and communities and draws on the author's experience of the development and delivery of a Common Awards Seedcorn Grant project aiming to equip people to minister in times of trauma. Chapter five explores theologies of trauma and their impact on ministry. In chapter six the focus on trauma and mission is developed further, identifying five key dimensions. Mission in times of trauma is: God focused, pastorally framed, trauma informed, liturgically held and creatively enabled. The final chapter looks at possible ways forward as we move through the impact of the COVID-19 pandemic and as we prepare for inevitable future trauma, whether personal, congregational, local, national or global.

2 Trauma and the Individual

The Nature and Impact of Trauma

Mary Oliver's poem *Treasures of Darkness* notes that she was once given a box that was full of darkness. It was only after the passage of years that she understood that this box, too, was a gift. Trauma is indeed a box of darkness, and for many the journey through to what is called post-traumatic growth—Mary Oliver's 'gift'—is hampered by a lack of informed, compassionate understanding and appropriate support to negotiate the journey of trauma.

'Traumatic events overwhelm the ordinary systems of care that give people a sense of control, connection and meaning.'[5] In his classic book on trauma, Bessel van der Kolk says, 'Trauma, by definition, is unbearable and intolerable.'[6] Trauma impacts on the whole person: body, mind, soul and heart. It 'results in a fundamental reorganization of the way mind and brain manage perceptions.'[7] It also interrupts the narrative of the person's life. Edith Eger, a psychotherapist working with traumatized war veterans and a survivor of Auschwitz, writes that she wishes she had known that she was not a damaged person, but that she was suffering from an interrupted life.[8] Trauma also has social impacts and often results in shame and distorted self-perception.

In a recent church study, death of a loved one, betrayal, domestic violence and physical and sexual abuse were identified as the most common traumatic experiences.[9] Trauma is not necessarily a one-off event. Long-term bullying and generational discrimination, for example racism, can be traumatic. The effects may be subtle but are corrosive. The trauma can be ongoing, unnoticed and unchecked for years until the experience is overwhelming, inescapable and unmanageable.

Towards a Definition

Honing down on a definition of trauma is not easy, but perhaps one of the better ones is that: '*A traumatic event is one in which a person or persons perceive themselves or others as threatened by an external force that seeks to annihilate them and against which they are unable to resist and which overwhelms their capacity to cope.*'[10]

Thus 'Traumatic events are extraordinary, not because they occur rarely, but rather because they overwhelm the normal human adaptations to life.'[11]

Trauma is made more likely by the traumatized person having been surprised, trapped or exposed to the point of exhaustion. 'When neither resistance nor escape is possible, the human system of self-defence becomes overwhelmed and disorganized.'[12] 'Traumatic events, by definition, thwart initiative and overwhelm individual competence. No matter how brave and resourceful the victim may have been her actions were insufficient to ward off disaster.'[13] Traumatic responses to adverse events are made more likely by traumatic events in childhood.[14]

In that trauma overwhelms, it impacts on the whole person. The brain does not handle traumatic memory the same as normal memory. It is therefore prone to being re-experienced as trauma if the unprocessed memory is triggered. This triggering results in the body responding automatically and the physical, emotional and spiritual impact of the trauma is revisited. This has been recognized for many years, and is now given the name Post-Traumatic Stress Disorder (PTSD).

Understanding the way individuals respond to trauma guides appropriate pastoral care.

It is in the Body

Trauma is held in the body, as the intricate detail of the nervous system that works beneath our conscious control responds to stressful stimuli. These processes are controlled by the *sympathetic* and *parasympathetic* parts of the nervous system that normally work together, rather like a couple dancing a waltz on a crowded dance floor. They respond and change with each other and in response to all the other things happening around them to keep equilibrium.

The parasympathetic part of the nervous system is responsible for bodily activity and responses when we rest, eat, digest food and respond sexually. The sympathetic part is responsible for our flight and fight responses. At rest, the sympathetic part is just ticking along in the background while the parasympathetic is more active. If the body notices something stressful happening the sympathetic part of the nervous system kicks in automatically and becomes more active, and the parasympathetic becomes less active. When this happens, our heart starts beating faster, our breathing becomes shallow and we get butterflies in our stomach as blood is diverted from the gut to the muscles. We become more alert. When the stressor goes, the sympathetic and parasympathetic rebound slightly and normalize. These stress responses are started by the release of adrenaline. The thinking part of the brain is bypassed while more subconscious processes seek to deal with the challenge at hand.

Trauma results in both sympathetic and parasympathetic parts of the nervous system behaving chaotically. When the sympathetic part takes priority, the body is moved into a 'fight' state of rage, anger and irritation or into a 'flight' state of panic, fear, anxiety and concern. When the person is overwhelmed and the parasympathetic takes priority, the body freezes with numbness, helplessness, dissociation and depression. The person can effectively shut down. The trauma reaction can cause patterns to develop in the unconscious part of the brain that make the person hypersensitive to future situations, which can repeatedly trigger the 'overwhelm' response in a way that the sufferer cannot control—PTSD.

Responses to Trauma

Appropriate early intervention promotes balanced responses and recovery from trauma. Unbalanced responses can result in the development of an acute or longer-term stress disorder. PTSD occurs when imbalance continues and where the person may re-experience the traumatic event with flashbacks, nightmares and intrusive thoughts. They may feel numb and try to avoid situations and places where memories are provoked. They may have periods of dissociation, memory lapses and times of apparently 'drifting off.' They may also experience hyperarousal and alertness.

Harmful coping strategies can then be adopted, for example using drugs and alcohol. Eating disorders and other mental health challenges may also develop, as might physical problems like insomnia, chronic pain, fibromyalgia and irritable bowel syndrome.

Initial bodily reactions to trauma can therefore include exhaustion, anxiety, confusion, sadness, numbness, dissociation and a flattened mood. Later reactions include sleep problems, ongoing tiredness, flashbacks, anxiety, depression and avoidant behaviour. These vary in severity and compromise well-being for some, but can be completely debilitating for others.

Recovery from Trauma

Models of recovery from trauma are still in their infancy, but do find resonance with models of grief and bereavement. They also have links with culture shock, learning and transition models. Serene Jones identifies three steps for recovery. Those who have experienced trauma need a safe place to *tell their story* and someone to witness their testimony. The person experiencing the trauma can then begin the process of *telling a new story*, and in doing this is able to pave a new pathway through the brain. This, Jones says, is not a forgetting of the past, but is about *meaning-making* and retelling the events in a way that agency is returned and hope becomes possible. She quotes Maya Angelou: 'History, despite its wrenching pain, cannot be unlived; but if faced with courage, it need not be lived again.'[15]

3 Trauma and Congregations

Trauma in congregations can take many forms. The compound loss of multiple deaths in elderly church communities can be experienced as trauma. One congregation and wider community over a period of time had to face a number of significant high-profile tragedies, including the death of one of its young people in a climbing accident; the death of another young person in a car crash; the imprisonment of the incumbent, choirmaster and the husband of one of the church members; a train disaster and the death of a link missionary in childbirth.

When congregations as a body see themselves threatened by something that they cannot control or resist, which overwhelms their ability to cope, they experience a traumatic response. While congregations do not have nervous systems in the way a body has, they do have ways of functioning that are affected by trauma. Kraus *et al* have mapped out the stages congregations go through.[16] The process typically takes about 18 months to 2 years.

Stage 1	*The Heroic Stage*. A phase of activity during which all who are able and want to help, seek to do so.
Stage 2	*The Disillusionment Stage*. Despite all the heroics, there is no return to normal. Lethargy and disillusionment creep in and begin to take over.
Stage 3	*Rock Bottom Stage*. Loss is accepted with an understanding that there will not be a return to normal. Instead there is a hope of a future different to what has been—a new normal.
Stage 4	*Rebuilding and Restoration Stage*. Tragedy is accepted, grief continues and there is positive engagement with the future that the congregation seeks to be part of, including times of remembering, dreaming and creativity.
Stage 5	*Wiser Living Stage*. Reminiscent of the apostle Paul's words, 'because we know that suffering produces perseverance; perseverance, character; and character, hope,' the congregation emerge older and wiser, having negotiated tragedy and trauma together (Rom 5.3–4).

The narrative of Noah illustrates these stages well. Stage one sees God telling Noah that he will destroy the earth. Noah and his family respond by building and boarding the ark. Stage two sees forty days and nights of rain. Stage three sees them afloat in the ark for one hundred and fifty days where the Earth is flooded with no sight of dry land. Stage four see the beginnings of hope as, in the seventh month, the ark lands on Ararat. The rebuilding and restoration phase of hope continues as the tops of mountains are seen and birds are sent out. Stage five sees Noah and his family come out of the ark, build an altar and sacrifice to the Lord, who blesses them and promises never again to destroy all living creatures.

A minister is arrested, goes to court and is given a custodial sentence. This is traumatic for all involved, including the congregation. The heroic stage might be about supporting the minister and their family, denying the charges, or standing in support around the victim. The disillusionment phase might be the realization that the minister, who may have been held on a pedestal, is human. Disillusionment here might hit as people feel let down by the person or the institution, or even their understanding of God. The rock bottom stage may be a recognition of the brokenness and sinfulness of all of humanity, including ministers and organizational church, but with an awareness and hope that God and God's church is bigger. This then leads on to the restoration and rebuilding stage, as the congregation moves towards a deeper and more realistic wisdom and understanding of what it means to be the body of Christ in the brokenness of the world.

Congregational responses to trauma vary

Congregational responses to trauma vary, as do the responses of individuals within each congregation. The COVID-19 pandemic has made this more complex, as many were drawn into multiple worshipping communities online that would not have been possible pre-COVID-19. While some felt the loss of sacramental ministry, others began to engage proactively with what future church might look like. While some wanted to 'return to Egypt,' others seemed to be running towards the new normal without taking time to learn the lessons of the desert. For some, strict lockdown became a place of retreat, for others a place of asking 'How long?' Dissentions arose between risk takers and risk avoiders as restrictions were eased, and holy communion emerged as an area of ongoing debate. But, while many hankered to get back into the church buildings and to return to 'before,' there was a growing congregational realization that there was no going back and that church would never be the same again. Something new, and better, would have to emerge.

4 Trauma and Communities

Texts on community trauma are significantly informed by the Holocaust. This event in history is one of many persecutions experienced by the Jewish people, but in its orchestrated efficiency—resulting in the deaths of over 6,000,000 Jewish people, and the annihilation of most of European Jewry and the Jewish way of life—it is unique. In it we see the impact of trauma on individuals and their descendants—communities scarred for life. The traumatic lessons of the Holocaust provide a framework for understanding other experiences of mass murder, for example in Rwanda and Cambodia, as well as the ongoing impact of historical and ongoing racism, abuse of women and discrimination against those with different abilities. They encourage us to consider the impact of direct and vicarious trauma experienced by those in healthcare, the armed services, emergency services and others who have seen the unseeable and heard the unhearable. They lead us to acknowledge the impact of trauma on the environment, both through significant events like Chernobyl and Hiroshima and the ongoing impact of environmental destruction.

In seeking to respond to community trauma we discern the missional call to *respond to human need by loving service*, to *transform unjust structures*, to *challenge violence of every kind*, to *seek peace and reconciliation* and to *safeguard the integrity of creation, sustaining and renewing the life of the Earth*. As with individual experiences of trauma, where knowing and growing in understanding of the bigger story enables return of agency and meaning-making, we recognize the call to contextually share the *good news of the kingdom*. Thus, the Church of England's Five Marks of Mission effectively describe good community trauma care.[17]

Church community structures, for example the parish, are predominantly geographical. If tragedy and trauma, such as flooding, hit a particular area, the local church is called to respond. An example of such a response is Churches Together in All Lincolnshire, which has developed a team of Emergency Faith Responders with the Lincolnshire Resilience Forum, who establish and maintain effective multi-agency emergency response. Faith responders are called up in times of tragedy and trauma to provide ministerial support.

Tragedy also hits communities in other ways. For example, the death of a teenager killed by a school bus will have a huge impact not only on the family and friends of the teenager, but also on the school and wider community.

It often resurrects memories of other untimely deaths that people have experienced. In the school itself, both friends of the teenager and staff grieve. While school pastoral care structures can access external professional help, this can take time. Good prior school—church relationships mean that the church is already present and, as well as practical pastoral help, a loving, purposeful, prayerful, pastoral presence can help hold the pain quietly, declaring the love of God and the bigger story.

The death of a baby in the community has an impact on family and friends, but can also vicariously affect the friends of the dead child's siblings at school, the members of a carers' and toddlers' group which the mother used to attend, the undertaker and healthcare professionals involved, and the many other people in the community who have previously directly or indirectly experienced baby death, miscarriage or abortion. The closure of a factory that employs a large number of local people is a tragedy that can be experienced as trauma not just for the individual, but for the community, as mass redundancies hit. The newspapers often headline other incidents that traumatize communities: a shooting, knife crime, flooding, rioting, arson and bombings.

The stages of response to trauma and tragedy in a community can be seen to reflect the stages in the congregational response, but the diversity of context needs consideration. In a congregation there is a history of gathering together. In a community this is not necessarily the case. While a whole town may be affected in some way by mass redundancy, the town is broken into smaller communities by nature of location, interest, age, background, employment, family and friends. While a school can enable the effective delivery of, and access to, appropriate support to school colleagues of the teenager killed by a bus, reaching children on the bus from other schools is more complex. The ongoing nature of community trauma is another complicating factor. Many of those affected by the burning down of the Grenfell Tower were still waiting, months later, for permanent housing and the ever-changing landscape of COVID-19 has resulted in repeated significant experiences of trauma through financial strain, job losses and separation from friends and family.

The church, as part of a community, has an essential and significant role to play by enabling the community to walk through trauma as the church holds and declares the bigger, meaning-making, redemptive story. This requires the church to be prepared practically and theologically for ministry and mission in times of trauma: to know its role, its people and its partners; to be able to prioritize and deal with practicalities and to have a vision for pastoral care that is fully and responsively integrated into the mission and ministry of the church. With an eye on the bigger picture, wisdom about boundaries and self-care, and reflectiveness and reflexivity in approach, all embedded in prayer, we are enabled wisely, graciously and humbly to follow the lead of the shepherd.

5 Trauma Theology

Towards a Theology of Trauma

Theodicy is about God and his justice and considers how God can allow suffering to take place. A theology of trauma explicitly seeks to bring God into our thinking about trauma. As a result, any church seeking to minister and be missional in times of trauma is helped by having already grappled with the philosophical problem of God and evil. This does not demand trite or overly complex answers as we turn into different shades of Job's comforters. Instead it requires deep consideration of a God who suffers in Jesus Christ, so that we have a framework through which we can begin to hold and share our limited but growing understanding.

Suffering is often seen as an outcome of two categories of evil: *moral evil,* the consequence of our wrongdoing, and *natural evil,* which arises out of natural events. Links between the two are not precluded. Humanity's rape of the natural world does result in natural disaster. But how can we reconcile these forms of evil and suffering with belief in the Christian God?

Attributes of God

A good God would not want gratuitous suffering. An all-knowing God would have known suffering would exist before he created the world. An all-powerful God could have prevented this suffering. This, the atheist argues, is proof that the Christian God does not exist. As Christians we affirm that a good, all-powerful, all-knowing God does exist. We also acknowledge the evil we see in the suffering, tragedy and trauma of the world. How can we hold these beliefs together? As N T Wright suggests in *Evil and the Justice of God,* 'For the Christian, the problem is how to understand and celebrate the goodness and God-givenness of creation and how, at the same time, to understand and face up to the reality and seriousness of evil. It is easy to "solve" the problem by watering down one side of this or the other.'[18]

Theoretical Approaches to Suffering

The *free will* approach argues that unless we have a deterministic world where free will is an illusion, evil will exist. Free will is seen to be what makes living valuable but it comes at a cost. For some God is seen to have a duty to act to prevent all suffering. If this were to be the case, there would be no consequences of our harmful actions, yet free will requires a stable world with consequences of our good and evil actions. As Robin Gill says in his book *Why Does God Allow Suffering?*, 'This may not be the best possible world, but it may be the only world possible that could allow for the emergence of life possessing rational and moral choice.'[19]

Suffering is sometimes seen as a way to *test our faith and to help us grow in character*. This is echoed in Rom 5.3–4. It is described by Helen Keller, 'Character cannot be developed in ease and quiet. Only through experience of trial and suffering can the soul be strengthened, ambition inspired and success achieved.' It is emphasized by C S Lewis in *The Problem of Pain*, 'I have seen great beauty in some who were great sufferers...if the world is indeed a "vale of soul-making" it seems on the whole to be doing its work.'[20] Edith Eger writes, 'Our painful experiences aren't a liability—they're a gift. They give us perspective and meaning, an opportunity to find our unique purpose and our strength.'[21]

Suffering is sometimes seen as a consequence of people turning away from God, a punishment for a people who have turned away from God, echoing the fall of Israel from the heights in the time of David and Solomon to the exile in Babylon. While Tom Wright argues effectively against the view of pandemic as punishment, suffering is seen by some as a wake-up call echoing the words of the Old Testament prophets, 'Seek me and live.'[22] This, in a slightly nuanced way, has echoes of the famous quote from C S Lewis indicating that suffering is God's megaphone to a deaf world.[23]

Suffering is seen by some as a wake-up call

A further approach to the theology of suffering is about the bigger picture and the longer, eschatological story, possibly best summed up in the words of Sunny in the film *The Best Exotic Marigold Hotel*. He says, 'Everything will be all right in the end. So if it's not all right, it is not yet the end.' The Jewish people looked back at their history to help them trust him for the future. The Old Testament, says N T Wright, 'is written to tell the story of what God has done, is doing, and will do about evil.'[24] He adds, 'The gospels present us not simply with the historical framework for an essentially non-historical salvation, but with the story of God's action to deal with evil at every level by letting it do its worst to his own incarnate self.'[25]

The 'now and not yet' of the kingdom, which underlies this eschatological perspective, is another key element in our understanding, often paralleled as living in the time between D-Day and VE Day. Acknowledging that we are ignorant and cannot solve the problem of suffering in a simple way is a step into wisdom. Realizing that sin and evil lie at root in our own selves lends deeper understanding, but this is held in the sure and certain knowledge of the victory of Christ, the triumph of the cross. We respond to the call of the gospel to 'implement the victory of God in the world through suffering love,' knowing the full forgiveness of the God who wants to deliver us from evil.[26] We also remember that there is a day of judgment which John Dickson describes as 'God's pledge to wounded humanity that he hears their cries for justice, and will one day console them by bringing his justice to bear on every evil act.'[27]

Job helps us develop further understanding. Job is reminded of his limitations and of the immensity of God, his love and his provision. Personal agency impacts on both experience of, and recovery from, trauma. For those for whom the bigger picture is held by an omniscient, omnipotent, omnipresent God, suffering does not have the last word. The agency and power of God is echoed in Psalms 8, 19 and 139 and in Isa 55.8–9. As Os Guinness so aptly says, 'We always have sure and sufficient reasons for knowing why we can trust God, but do not always know what God is doing and why.'[28] But there is more. The psalmist in Psalm 23 notes the presence of God in the valley of the shadow of death. The suffering Christ brings another dimension to this: 'No other religion has this model of God identifying so deeply and so compassionately with humanity. We go through suffering not alone, but with God at our side.'[29] Immanuel. God is with us and shares our pain.

Immanuel. God is with us and shares our pain

In preparing the church for mission in times of trauma, enabling the development of a framework of understanding that can hold and, if necessary, adapt when trauma and tragedy hit, will enable us to say with Job, 'I know that my redeemer lives' (Job 19.25). Teaching and preaching a theology of suffering helps our congregations to prepare and live as mature Christians in a world of suffering, being aware that in many cases it is our congregations who, out of their experience, can teach us. We celebrate the good and we bewail the bad, but in it all are able to say, 'Blessed be God forever.'

Trauma and Lament

From the self-induced trauma of the ruptured relationship with God and the devastation of sin in the Genesis narrative, to the mass deaths with the flood in the time of Noah, to the destruction of Jerusalem and exile into Babylon, trauma, death and devastation in some shape or form permeate the OT narrative. Lament is also present. In Psalm 88, one of the lament psalms, there is no response by God to the psalmist's complaint: 'Why, Lord, do you reject me and hide your face from me?' Although hope is present in a brief glimpse, protest, lament and desperation also fill the Book of Lamentations, and can be seen in the cries and complaints of the prophet in Habakkuk. 'I lament therefore I am' could be seen to be an existential subtext to some of these passages. Scripture shows us that lament needs to have an expression and a voice, and that voice needs to be heard. Lament has a healing function. It is acknowledged in trauma care that relating the trauma narrative in a safe, witnessed space is a key part of the healing process. This is not forgetting the past. It is re-narrating the events in such a way that promotes agency, reframing and meaning-making. Hope becomes possible.

In this way, unprocessed memories can begin to be processed. Meaning can be made from the suffering. While this does not let the perpetrators off the hook for inflicting suffering, it does release the victim from victimhood. Lament is necessary and cannot be rushed. We compromise and prevent healing and transformation by insisting on a rapid return to an old but empty normal, at the cost of the longer journey into a transformed, deeper and more complete new normal.

In the psalms, we see movement from trauma to healing in action. The psalmist laments. Once lament has run its course there is a turning point, usually centred around the greatness of God and his agency. Choice, a decision of the will follows: 'Yet I will praise you.' As the words of Hab 3.18 illustrate, though adversity happens '...yet I will rejoice in the Lord, I will be joyful in God my Saviour.' Psalm 13 has a similar turning point when in response to the lament 'How long?,' the psalmist sings, 'But I trust in your unfailing love; my heart rejoices in your salvation.'

In the words of John Dickson:

> In the great work of art we call the universe, I cannot always follow the hand of the Artist: some of his work just eludes me. But what the biblical narrative tells me—and, in particular the account of Christ's passion—is that while I may not be able to trace the Artist's hands at all times, I can always trust his motives. The God who is in control of all things, who acts behind the scenes in all things, is also the God who willingly suffers. He is the one I can shout at, cry with and find comfort in. His heart, if not all his ways, is clear to me because on the cross he wore it on his sleeve for all to see.[30]

Creating space for individual, congregational and communal lament is essential.

6 Trauma and Mission

'When the church becomes a place of healing we won't have to go out and persuade people to come in; our problem will be finding time to deal with all who want to come.'[31] The church as a place of healing lives out a deeply intertwined marriage of mission and ministry for the glory of God. Outlined in the five marks of mission this ministry is God-focused, pastorally framed, trauma-informed, liturgically held and creatively approached.

God-focused

It is all about God's glory and about him being enjoyed forever. As we worship, others are also drawn into worship. Once the good news of Jesus truly takes hold of us, we are transformed and people are drawn by what they see of God in us. Therefore, as we follow the call of the master, all we are and all we do will be a sharing of the good news. As others see more of God and less of us, so the allure of the gospel will be more at work, as people are drawn out of the desert to hear the tender words of God leading them into new life in Christ.

God-focused mission in times of trauma starts with us in worship. We must first dig deep into God—this is the ultimate form of self-care. The fourth degree of Bernard of Clairvaux's degrees of love is about loving ourselves for God's sake. Self-care is not about marking out time in the diary to do things to help us recover from the rest of life only to return to the rest of life to be harmed again. True self-care comes out of our love relationship with God, where we are not driven by the desire for approval or acclaim or acceptance, but are drawn into an ever-deeper love relationship with God that permeates our being itself, our every breath and action. While forms of worship may change, to be missional communities and congregations in times of trauma we must remain God-focused.

During the COVID-19 pandemic, the initial drive of churches was to make congregational worship accessible online. Resources were prepared to help people alone in lockdown draw near to God, knowing that they were being held as individuals, congregations and the wider community. Worship playlists were sent out and shared. Virtual prayer stations, prayer rooms, online retreats and online accompanied prayer and reflections were made available. Many of these were shared with those on the edge of or outside the institutional church. While we can minister to others in our brokenness and, as Ecclesiastes reminds us, we can help pick each other up when traversing the journey through trauma, as we come close to God, what shines out of us in our brokenness is the light of Christ.

Pastorally Framed

The *pastoral framing* of mission is particularly important in times of trauma. Different people resonate with different models of pastoral care—a common one being the various pictures of the good shepherd.

God's expectation in Ezekiel 34 is that shepherds will care for the sheep and not just feed themselves. He expects them to strengthen the weak, to heal the sick and bind up the injured. They are to bring back the strays and search for the lost. God describes himself as that model shepherd who looks after the scattered flock and brings them back from where they are scattered on a day of clouds and darkness. He tends and feeds them in good pasture so that they lie down. Pastoral care is missional. It is not just about care of the gathered flock. It is about searching for the scattered, the hungry, the sick, the broken and the weak. And it is then about binding up, tending, feeding and healing so that they can lie down and rest.

Seven 'C's of pastoral care bring focus in times of trauma: care, compassion, comfort, consolation, connection, community—and a commitment to make it happen. Practical care, driven by hearts of compassion as the good shepherd cares for us with his heart of compassion; the desire and willingness to comfort and console as we too have been comforted and consoled; connection and community, not just with others in the neighbourhood, whatever that may be, but for a connection with the bigger story that means that trauma does not have the last word.

In the disillusionment phase of trauma response, Kraus emphasizes the importance of truth in bringing freedom.[32] Establishing the real state of the congregation and wider community, for example through appreciative enquiry, is beneficial. In times of trauma, church missional narratives are interrupted and context requires a rethinking of what, when, who and how. *In times of trauma, mission is trauma-informed pastoral care as the why of the big story of the Good News is proclaimed, human need is served, people are nurtured in adversity, unjust structures are challenged and life is renewed.*

In times of trauma, mission is trauma-informed pastoral care

Who the scattered sheep are will vary depending on the trauma; and the ability to reach them will depend on the roads and bridges already in place. Temporary makeshift bridges can be built that may in time become substantive. With the teenager killed by a school bus, prior relationship with the teenager or their family will open the door to giving care, which may include funeral ministry. Prior relationships with the school they attended might enable being part of a team putting in place structures and liturgies to tend, care for and bind up the wounded, including the school staff. Links with local, regional or diocesan teams with relevant wisdom and experience might increase the resources and expertise available. An effective funeral ministry team, with structured follow-up, will enable a longer journey moving from immediate to longer-term care as wounds get bound up and begin to heal. All of this is mission as we reach out and help God to gather those who are suffering into his arms. Ministerial vulnerability, collegiality, fellowship, support and supervision are needed.

Organizations like Open[33] and Loved minister to those who have lost babies through miscarriage and abortion and help churches run services which enable those who have experienced baby loss to gather, remember and give voice to or symbolize the loss.[34] They enable those attending to be tended and ministered to in the ongoing process of healing and binding up of wounds. At one such service, over Baby Loss Awareness Week, a national flower-growing company offered long-stemmed white roses for those attending to take away. The church congregation as a whole prayed for the service, which was advertised in the wider community. Over half those attending were men and over half were non-churchgoers. This is missional pastoral care in a time of trauma—where that trauma may be decades old or more recent—that aims to enable people to receive the deep wholeness and healing that only God can give.

During the COVID-19 pandemic, pastoral care took many forms

During the COVID-19 pandemic, pastoral care took many forms. Communities sought volunteers. Experts in trauma, change and transition were recruited to frame events and identify support pathways. Spiritual, emotional and practical support was required by those at the coal face. Churches organized phone-call care, delivery of food and small gifts to encourage. Schools wanted resources. Devotional resources were shared, while online church services enabled those on the edge to join in and be part of a wider community. Voluntary Christian organizations offered free counselling.

Normally those working with people who are experiencing trauma have supervision. Pastorally framed mission in times of trauma is further enabled by pastoral supervision for ministers and pastoral care teams by providing safe places for theological reflection, consideration of self-care and addressing vicarious trauma.

Trauma-Informed

Mission in times of trauma is *trauma-informed*. This includes noticing what trauma is being experienced. This is often obvious. In the COVID-19 pandemic, death and illness impacted on many directly and indirectly through loss of contact with others, loss of employment and financial strain. What was more hidden included increased domestic violence; women pressurized to have home abortions; parents of children with behavioural challenges left feeling unsupported. At times of trauma, as in war, it is often the rich who make the decisions and the poor who pay with their lives. Trauma can exacerbate inequalities, the increased death rate of BAME communities from COVID-19 being a significant example. Trauma also has longer-term impacts. Many recovering from COVID-19 have ongoing compromised health. The delay in other important but non-emergency service provision impacts on those with cancer, heart disease and other chronic conditions. The prolonged nature of the impact of COVID-19, including economic and psychological trauma, can result in mental illness and burnout.

Trauma-informed mission enables a *moving through the journey of trauma*. This includes providing a safe place for the stories of trauma—of individuals, of congregations and of communities—to be heard and witnessed. In the case of the teenager killed by a bus this might include being available to listen not just to the students but also to the staff. It might be about creating a memorial prayer space or book. It may well include seeing the funeral as a way of creating safe spaces for the family and friends and community to express their pain. At the funeral of one young man, all those attending were invited to write on the cardboard coffin prior to the burial, giving space and witness to loss and lament.

Mission in times of trauma recovery is contextual

Mission in times of trauma recovery is contextual. *Attention to detail* can prevent compounding the trauma. Over All Souls, many churches have a service where families come to give thanks and remember their loved ones who have died. People who only come to church at this time of year come to hear their pain named as the names of their loved ones are read out. Here mission in times of trauma includes an obsessive focus in making sure no name is missed off the list and having a compassionate safety net in case one is.

Mission in times of trauma enables *reframing and making of meaning*. At the All Souls service, people often perform some symbolic action that helps reframe the loss and give meaning, for example by lighting a candle or taking away a bulb to plant. These are also powerful metaphors of gospel hope.

Mission in times of trauma returns agency as people put their trust in the ultimate agency of God. This good news story is essential to help re-narrate the events in such a way that agency is restored, but the story benefits from being shared in a trauma-informed way and not rushed. The seeds are scattered so that when the time is right, they can take root in the traumatized person, congregation and community and bring forth healing and fruit in due season.

Liturgically Held

> Worship is the place where the work of lament, the grieving of losses, and the expressions of anger and hope are held in holy tenderness...The liturgy and rituals of faith hold the story of the congregation together and provide the creative form that broods over brokenness and brings healing shape to the chaos of trauma and its aftermath.[35]

Liturgy is missional and liturgy is pastoral care. In the initial stages of trauma, after ensuring effective self-care and support is in place, ministry is stabilized. This is not about giving answers or about heroic overactivity, but about being present to God as well as family, congregation and community.

The rituals of worship provide a place for the stories of trauma to be heard and witnessed. The salvation story moving from brokenness to lament to restoration declares the bigger picture. The psalms in their move from orientation to disorientation through to reorientation lend themselves to help people journey through trauma.[36] In the psalms of deliverance, the sovereignty, power and agency of God are demonstrated. In the aftermath of the disillusionment phase of trauma the psalms of lament can give voice to the unspeakable and organize the remembering. Encouraging people to write a personal or communal psalm of lament can be cathartic and healing. In the recovery to a new normal, the psalms of lament give way to the psalms of thanksgiving. Those who have sown in tears reap with songs of joy (Psalm 126).

Congregations can be held through the liturgy of words, music, art and other creative liturgical approaches. In this there is care, connection and community. For some this might be a simple lighting of a candle in church. During COVID-19, this was demonstrated for some with the placing of a candle in the window each Sunday evening. Communities can also be held liturgically in very similar ways, where prior relationships and networks offer opportunities and as new opportunities emerge.

As the congregation journey through the trauma, the liturgy provides a place of worship, openness and safety for those who would normally be there but also for those drawn to God and the gathered worshipping community as a result of the trauma. Kraus describes three necessary stages of worship in the aftermath of trauma: *letting go* of what was and seeking sanctuary in the presence of God; *letting be* in being present to one another in the distress and *letting begin* as the walk out of the valley of the shadow begins. This approach also translates over to the wider community, whether a local church school, a community gathering in the wake of trauma, or in one-to-one relationships.

In both congregational and community contexts, frameworks for journeying through trauma to recovery find resonance in Scripture, for example in narratives of flood, exodus, exile and Holy Week. The trauma of Good Friday and the grief and hope of Holy Saturday lead to new life and resurrection. Thus, not only does liturgy allow voice and witness, it reframes the story—it is Friday, but Sunday is coming.

For many regular churchgoers, a familiar liturgy is both comfortable and comforting. It can, however, hold out a false hope of a return to normal rather than encouraging a looking forward to a new normal, reminiscent of the Israelites wanting to return to Egypt. Moving forward to the promised land can sometimes be modelled by doing something new and different with liturgy. Informal services and memorial services in times of trauma which are word-poor and symbol-rich can often minister profoundly. Gatherings for contemplative prayer and guided theological reflection can create connection and community.

Over COVID-19, churches sought a variety of ways to enable liturgy to hold the people of God in times of trauma. Often this aimed to include other members of the watching household, those who would not normally go to a church service, to become part of the worshipping community and to be introduced to the shepherd who walks with them through the valley of the shadow of death. The invitation to a holy space itself can be part of the healing journey through trauma. In a school where a child has died, an invitation to a service of light communicates that there is a light even in the darkness of trauma.

Creatively Approached

> Trauma provokes affective numbing and 'psychic closing off' which limits the freedom of creative expression. Conversely, creativity can provide a powerful escape from an inescapable traumatic situation. Later in development, creativity may be engaged as a potent modality for healing the wounds inflicted during the traumatic relational interactions; however, alterations in brain structure and function may need to be addressed during the healing process.[37]

Mission in times of trauma is creative. While it has been noted that prose under pressure becomes poetry, words sometimes are not enough, and they can be too much. In healthcare, creativity is integral to trauma therapy. Trauma is held in the body and healing takes place at this level as well. Imagination, symbol and ritual can be part of this. Holy Communion is a key example. Over COVID-19, the inability of people to receive communion became a trauma amplifier. The development of contemplative approaches to fill this gap could not replace the physicality of breaking, eating and drinking that is in itself healing. Communion is multisensory, involving taste, touch, smell, sight and hearing. It is in the body.

The use of poetry, image, music and art, praying with stuff, Bible art journaling, intercessional prayer cairns, gratitude collages, bread making, are all in the body and can open the door to the healing work of the Spirit. Over COVID-19, the author of this booklet created daily interactive prayer stations using *Lectio Divina*, Ignatian prayer, image, poetry, music and other creative approaches to prayer. The stations were God-focused, trauma-informed, pastorally framed, liturgically held and creatively approached and designed for sharing with church attenders and those on the edge. In the evangelical tradition, praying with beads is often reacted against, and yet prayer bracelets which encourage the person to pray the Lord's Prayer or Psalm 23 or the Serenity prayer have been valued by many of different denominations. Creative spaces to enable people to meet with God are both mission and ministry and can be adapted to group demography—woodwork, metalwork, clay and pyrography are often popular with men. In times of trauma, an intentionality about providing such space for being in the body and receiving God's healing is ministry and mission in action.

The Way Forward

7

In times of trauma, the body of Christ seeks God's heart to understand those times and, remembering that God works in all things with and through those who love him, seeks to know what to do. In answering the questions *What needs to be done here? Who is most at risk? How can we help? Who shall we send?*, the whole body of Christ, as the men of Issachar (I Chronicles 12.32), is enabled to fulfil its calling.

It is all about grace. 'The church is called, as it exists in this space of trauma, to engage in the crucial task of reordering the collective imagination of its people and to be wise and passionate in this task. As a people of faith, the church enables us to be story tellers, weavers, artists, poets, and visionaries who take the repetitive violence of 9/11 and reframe it in the context of the story of our faith.'[38] The church has the ability and vocation to be those story tellers as it engages pastorally in times of trauma with a missional perspective. As well as addressing the more obvious needs in times of trauma we are also 'called to help write the scripts of the Christian imagination as it seeks to bring order to this disorder, and we must do so in a manner that seeks the flourishing of all people.'[39]

And there is no other story that can do this but the story of Jesus, as crystallized on the road to Emmaus. The disciples are traumatized. Jesus gives them a safe space to narrate the trauma, and have it witnessed. He then proceeds to tell them the story of salvation and thereby reframes the trauma—there is meaning-making. And then in the gathering at the table this process of restoring from trauma is embodied in the breaking of bread.

The church has a missional call in times of trauma. To fulfil this call, and to address the questions of 'What?' 'Who?' and 'How?' requires:

Prayer—is the church a people of prayer, walking at the heels of the shepherd?

Preparation—is the church prepared theologically for suffering and trauma, building on prior community links prepared for such a time as this? This is facilitated by a trauma toolkit ready at short notice including essential phone numbers.[40] The ministers benefit from an ongoing supportive relationship with peers, a pastoral supervisor and spiritual director.

People—do the church members, leaders and community know their roles and who else to involve and alert? Does the church need to recruit and gather more people for missional ministry at this time? Who is speaking to the press?

Place—what is the church's locus of ministry and how has this changed with the trauma? Should the church or other church building be open, and if so for what? If not, what other places should or could be available in the real or virtual world? Where will people gather and what hospitality is required? Might the church be present in another place of hospitality as guests rather than hosts?

Partnership—who are the partners at this time? What diocesan, regional or national church partners are there? What links are there with Churches Together? What are the partnerships with schools, emergency services, local councils?

Priorities—what are the priorities? Is this about beds and food in the church building or establishing an online worshipping community? Is this about presence in a school along with the school pastoral team, or is it creating a reflective space with candles and a book of remembrance?

Practicalities—where / what / how / who / when? Who is best placed to organize these practicalities and how can they be sustained?

Pastoral care—what pastoral care is required and by whom, both in the acute phase and the longer term? How are care, compassion, comfort, consolation, connection and community best enabled in the longer and short term? What are the care and supervision structures for the carers and how is self-care going to be enabled? How is commitment going to be sustained for the long run?

Pastoral leadership—who are the leadership team and what are their roles and responsibilities? How can the leadership team act as role models and inform culture? What are the lines of communication?

Perspective—how is the larger and longer story being told, shared, held and embodied by the people of God?

Protection—have appropriate risk assessments been done and addressed? Have safeguarding issues been fully considered and addressed? What are the boundary issues at play? Is there a press-free zone?

Processing—how is time for individual reflection and review being structured? Where is the supervision coming from? How best are those involved going to watch and wait? What else is wanted? What learning needs to be shared and with whom?

8 Concluding Remarks

For the church, a time of trauma could be a time of creative, compassionate mission. It is a time where the church uses the abilities and experiences of people who are gifted in diverse ways to help guide and inspire those who feel uncertain. Diocesan, regional and national teams can be key resources to those in local church at this time. It is a time for sharing wisdom and resources as we seek to be the people of God in the world. The 12 'P's listed above help us address practicalities and structures.

There are a few key things to remember. Trauma needs time for lament—this is something that the church can hold and speak into. It is a time for compassion and care—this the church is placed to minister. It is a time for the bigger story to be known—the church holds that bigger story. It is all about grace—a grace that needs to be shared. And it is about the light shining in the darkness—this is the church's calling.

Notes

1 Tom Wright, *God and the Pandemic* (London: SPCK, 2020) pp 34–35.

2 Diane Langberg, *Suffering and the Heart of God* (Greensboro, NC: New Growth Press, 2015) p 8.

3 Viktor E Frankl, *Man's Search for Meaning* (New York: Washington Square Press, 1985) p 101.

4 https://tragedyandcongregations.org.uk/

5 Judith Herman, *Trauma and Recovery* (New York: Basic Books, 1992) p 33.

6 Bessel van der Kolk, *The Body Keeps the Score* (London: Random House, 2014) p 1.

7 *ibid*, p 21.

8 Edith Eger, *The Choice* (New York: Scribner, 2017) p 174.

9 Barna, *Trauma in America* (Barna Resources, 2020).

10 In Serene Jones, *Trauma and Grace* (Louisville, KY: Westminster John Knox, 2019) p 13.

11 Herman, *op cit*, p 33.

12 *ibid*, p 34.

13 *ibid*, p 53.

14 https://bit.ly/2DFfkQj

15 Jones, *op cit*, p 32.

16 Laurie Kraus, *Recovering from Un-Natural Disasters* (Louisville, KY: Westminster John Knox, 2017).

17 https://www.peterborough-diocese.org.uk/menu-church-resources/five-marks-of-mission-and-the-five-values-of-a-missionary-church

18 N T Wright, *Evil and the Justice of God* (London: SPCK, 2006) p 20.

19 Robin Gill, *Why Does God Allow Suffering?* (London: SPCK, 2015) pp 22–23.

20 C S Lewis, *The Problem of Pain* (London: Fontana, 1959) p 96.

21 Eger, *op cit*, p 314.

22 Wright, *God and the Pandemic, op cit,* pp 15–17.

23 Lewis, *op cit*, p 81.

24 Wright, *Evil and the Justice of God, op cit,* pp 23–24.

25 *ibid*, p 64.

26 *ibid*, p 62.

27 John Dickson, *If I were God, I'd End All the Pain* (Kingsford, Australia: Matthias Media, 2002) p 47.

28 Os Guinness, *God in the Dark* (Wheaton, IL: Crossway, 1996) p 168.

29 Philip Yancey, *The Question that Never Goes Away* (London: Hodder and Stoughton, 2013) p 75.

30 Dickson, *op cit*, p 67.

31 Cecil Kerr in Morris Maddocks, *A Healing House of Prayer* (London: Hodder and Stoughton, 1995) p 100.

32 Kraus, *op cit*, pp 50–51.

33 http://www.weareopen.org.uk/

34 https://www.weareopen.org.uk/wp-content/uploads/2020/04/Care-UK-Loved-Brochure-2020.pdf

35 Kraus, *op cit*, p 43.

36 Walter Brueggemann, *Praying the Psalms* (Eugene, OR: Wipf and Stock, second edition, 2007).

37 http://www.healingresources.info/article_thomson1.htm

38 Jones, *op cit*, p 31.

39 *ibid.*

40 https://www.tragedyandcongregations.org.uk/wp-content/uploads/TRAUMA-RESPONSE-TOOLKIT.pdf